P9-BYK-658

Listen to Your Fish

Terrific Tips for Pet Care

By Sarah Albee
Illustrated by Tom Brannon

"Sesame Workshop"®, "Sesame Street"®, and associated characters, trademarks, and design elements are owned and licensed by Sesame Workshop. ©2003, 2011 Sesame Workshop. All Rights Reserved.

Published by Dalmatian Press, 2011, an imprint of Dalmatian Publishing Group, Franklin, Tennessee 37067. No part of this book may be reproduced or copied in any form without written permission from the copyright owner. 1-866-418-2572

Printed in China

CE12919/0111/ZHE

Hello there, boys and girls! It is I, Grover, here to tell you my nine "Dos and Don'ts" for taking care of pets!

The most important thing about choosing a pet—whether it is a cute doggie, fish, or llama—is that it should be the right animal for YOUR family. Wild animals LOOK cute and adorable but do not make good pets.

Are you ready for Grover's nine rules for taking care of pets? Turn the page for Rule #1!

Excuse me,
sir, but I seem to have
lost my sheep.
Leave them alone,
and they'll come
home.
Mom, she
followed me home.
Can we keep her?

Pet Rule #1: Do give your pet fresh food and clean water every day.

Hey, no problem, Fluffy.
We can play later.

Pet Rule #2: **Do make sure your pet gets regular checkups at the veterinarian.**

Pet Rule #3: Do be sure your pet gets exercise every day.

Pet Rule #4: **Do help your pet stay clean and well-groomed.**

Pet Rule #5: Do not feed pets food from your plate.

It not healthy for them! It teaches pets bad eating habits, like begging for food, which me know is not polite.
Oh, look! Cookies for dessert!
Gimme, gimme, gimme! Please, oh, please, gimme COOOOOOOOKIES!!!

Pet Rule #6: Do not go near strange dogs . . . or crocodiles.

Pet Rule #7: **Do keep your pet on a leash in public places.**

Leashes help keep dogs from getting into fights with other dogs.

Pet Rule #8: Do be gentle with your pet.
Be sure to watch little babies carefully when they are around pets. Even nice pets might get angry if someone is rough with them.

And remember to wash your hands after you pet your pet.

Pet Rule #9: **Do give your pet lots of love and attention.**

I didn't know where to find you! But you all came home, wagging your tails behind you.

And so, boys and girls, if you remember your friend Grover's nine rules, you will have a happy and healthy pet. Down, kitties! Good kitties. Nice kitties . . .
Pet Rule #10: Do expect a lot of attention from cats after rolling around in catnip.
Maybe you need one more pet rule, Mister Grover.